D0576058

LUCI SWINDOLL

Quite Honestly

with
CARLA BECK   Creative Director

A journal of thoughts and activities
for daily living

Zondervan Publishing House
Grand Rapids, Michigan

QUITE HONESTLY
Copyright © 1989 by Luci Swindoll

Daybreak Books are published by
Zondervan Publishing House
1415 Lake Drive, S.E.
Grand Rapids, MI 49506
ISBN 0-310-51790-7

Edited by Nia Jones
Designed by Carla Beck

Printed in the United States of America

89 90 91 92 93 94 / DW / 39 38 37 36 35 34

Dear Friends,

How does one title a book like this? I didn't want to call it "Diary." That's sort of like Tarzan and Jane naming their son "Boy." It had to be better than that. It's not really a notebook because you can't add or subtract pages. Almanac doesn't fit . . . there are no home remedies, garden tips, household hints, or horoscopes.

I was discussing this problem with Carla, the creative director of this project. After many hours of brainstorming possibilities and tossing out most of them, she said, "Luci, you've got to decide what to title this thing. We can't do too much with it 'til we have some sort of theme."

"All right. All right. But quite honestly, I don't know what to call it. It's just a journal of. . . ."

"Hang on!" she yelled. "That's it: Quite Honestly! That's perfect. It's a journal of honest feedback, of what a person does and thinks over a year's time." (Sometimes, the trivia that falls from our lips has some value.)

That is precisely what this book is all about. It's your opportunity to be open and honest with yourself—every day, if you like.

Actually, the whole thing is what *you* make it. It's your chance to tell it like it is. You can laugh or cry throughout these pages. You can confess hidden secrets. You can remember that special date when you look at your saved ticket stubs. You can record significant events during your year or talk about everyday stuff. You can reveal your past and plan your future. You can design clothes. You can argue with various newspaper clippings you've read and cut out. You can chart your vacation and a trip abroad. You can compose songs, poetry, essays. You can draw pictures or paste in snapshots. You can skate the surface of your feelings, or you can pour out your deepest hurts, joys, longings all over these pages. You can even, as George Burns jokingly says, ". . . learn to fake sincerity. Once you master that, you've got it made." Quite honestly, this book will be whatever you want it to be. It will reflect you.

Before you get into it, however, I want to point out a few things that you'll probably notice anyway. There is no year and there are

no days of the week shown anywhere. That's on purpose, so that if you want, you can buy copies annually until the end of time and use *this very journal* year after year. Just fill up one and begin a new one 365 days later. Also, note that at the end of each month there's a place for re-capping. You're going to like that because, in a nutshell, you'll be able to see all you've accomplished over the past 28 or 29 or 30 or 31 days. You'll also recognize the areas that need a little beefing up.

Then hold onto your hat! At the end of 365 days, it'll be easy to re-cap your whole year by simply reading all your monthly re-cap notes and writing that information in the "Year-End Re-cap" I've provided. You'll have so much fun at the beginning of the new year when people ask, "What are *your* New Year's resolutions?" and you'll say, "Well, I'm working on those now based on some of the things I accomplished last year. Would you believe, I lost 30 pounds? I saved $200. I memorized 25 verses. I coached a basketball team, and I read *War and Peace*. I even kept a journal. How 'bout them apples?"

If they're still awake, you can announce your plans for going to the moon in a spacecraft, or roller skating from Houston to Dallas in the coming year. You never know what new ideas will develop as you write and dream.

Because Carla and I are both kids at heart, we decided to design these pages so you can add stickers if you want. It's that touch of whimsy here and there that will spice up your comments. Just peel them off and add zest where you're trying to make a point. If you can't find the right sticker, but you need an illustration, draw a picture. It doesn't have to be good or make sense. Just think of Picasso and draw away!

There is no magic in keeping a journal. There's no big secret of how to do it. When you don't feel like writing, don't write. Sometimes we're not in the mood. I've been journaling for a number of years now, and I like it more all the time. When I first started, I thought, *Gosh, all those blank pages . . . I'll never fill this thing up.* But I learned that the object is not to fill a book with words. The object is to express what I'm thinking and/or doing. I've had gaping, empty spots during certain weeks of writing and other weeks when there wasn't enough room to say all I wanted to say. That's the way we are. Sometimes we're verbal; sometimes we're not. So, don't worry if nothing flows—you don't have to write every day. But when it does, try your best to capture with a pen everything that's in your well of thoughts. Proverbs 20:5 reads, "Counsel in the heart of a man is like deep water." It's that deep water you're hoping to tap because therein lies your counsel.

Therein lies the *real* you. Saying what you really feel gives a tremendous sense of relief.

I have assigned themes to the twelve months:

January: Beauty	July: Freedom
February: Friends	August: Travel
March: Achievements	September: Books
April: Faith	October: Solitude
May: Music	November: Hospitality
June: Laughter	December: Celebrations

These are my favorite discussion topics in life, and tied to each one are quotations I hope will encourage you. They are taken either from the five books I've written or from a book called *Soloing*, which I edited for Fleming Revell Company. If you find you have an overwhelming urge to rush out and buy one of these books, please don't hesitate. I'll make it easy for you by listing them here:

Wide My World, Narrow My Bed (Multnomah Press)

The Alchemy of the Heart (Multnomah Press)

My Favorite Verse (Accent Books)

You Bring the Confetti (Word, Inc.)

After You've Dressed for Success (Word, Inc.)

Before I run along and let you begin your chronicle of musings and events, let me thank you for buying this book. I truly hope it will be a source of joy, information, and refreshment for you in the coming year.

Thanks also to my wonderful friend, Carla Beck, whose creative flair helped put this journal into shape. We've been wanting to do a project together for a couple years, and we finally did it. Yippee!! To my attentive secretary, Patty Elam, my sincere appreciation for her kindness in typing the quotations and this letter you're now reading. And, finally, I want to express my thanks to Terry Jenkins, the graphic designer who was invaluable with his artistic talent and critical eye.

Okay. I'm outa here. Have fun! I hope you'll thoroughly enjoy "writing your own book" in the days ahead. Dazzle (and surprise) yourself with talent you never dreamed possible. And, when the year ends, look back through this journal with a smile and savor the sense of accomplishment you will have earned . . . quite honestly.

Yours for the joy of living,

Luci Swindoll

With affection, this book is
dedicated to the first individual
I knew personally who kept a journal
and encouraged me to do the same,
my wonderful and imaginative friend:
Kurt Ratican
Here's to twenty-five years of love
and friendship.

JANUARY

Beauty

Beauty brings magic and joy
as it transforms and transfigures.

You Bring the Confetti, page 130

ACTIVITIES

1

2

3

4

5

6

7

JANUARY

THOUGHTS

A real person's beauty
comes from being in tune with God.

Soloing, page 20

ACTIVITIES

8

9

10

11

12

13

14

JANUARY

THOUGHTS

Who can predict what will stir our hearts or move our spirits?
Often, it is that which we least expect,
hidden within the larger context of something else.

You Bring the Confetti, page 137

ACTIVITIES

15

16

17

18

19

20

21

THOUGHTS

Notably present in a true professional are "quality of life" attributes—
tranquility, warmth, wisdom, peace, humor, imagination—
these are the issues of the heart. They make us beautiful.

After You've Dressed for Success, page 51

ACTIVITIES

22

23

24

25

26

27

28

JANUARY

THOUGHTS

There is so much beauty around us
if we only take the time to notice.
You Bring the Confetti, page 140

ACTIVITIES

29

30

31

RE-CAP

FEBRUARY

Friends

There is no doubt about it,
faithful friends are treasures indeed,
and I thank God for those He has given to me.

The Alchemy of the Heart, page 84

ACTIVITIES

1

2

3

4

5

6

7

FEBRUARY

THOUGHTS

Friends unconsciously teach us a lot about living,
simply because of what we feel for them and what they feel for us.
To put it briefly, that's what friends are for.

The Alchemy of the Heart, page 83

ACTIVITIES

8

9

10

11

12

13

14

FEBRUARY

THOUGHTS

Truthfulness is a quality of value in friendship I admire greatly,
and one which Solomon lauds in Proverbs 27:6:
"Wounds from a friend are better than kisses from an enemy."
The Alchemy of the Heart, page 84

ACTIVITIES

15

16

17

18

19

20

21

FEBRUARY

THOUGHTS

Supportive friends and colleagues are among our most important assets—
they are vital to our emotional, mental, and spiritual health.

After You've Dressed for Success, page 103

ACTIVITIES

22

23

24

25

26

27

28

Having friends adds such sweetness to life.
"Friendship is tenderness," Emerson says.
Wide My World, Narrow My Bed, page 119

29

RE-CAP

MARCH

Achievements

There is something in each one of us
that makes us want to measure development or record change—
especially if it's positive.

The Alchemy of the Heart, page 12

ACTIVITIES

1

2

3

4

5

6

7

MARCH

THOUGHTS

All of our accomplishments are made possible
by the grace and provision of God.
You Bring the Confetti, page 114

ACTIVITIES

8

9

10

11

12

13

14

MARCH

THOUGHTS

To achieve future rewards, we must learn that everything cannot be had now.
The richest life has a lot of waiting in it . . .
a present investment for future fulfillment.

After You've Dressed for Success, page 58

ACTIVITIES

15

16

17

18

19

20

21

MARCH

THOUGHTS

Remember, you wouldn't be where you are now
if you hadn't set your sights toward a goal
and continued to strive for that mark.
You Bring the Confetti, page 115

ACTIVITIES

22

23

24

25

26

27

28

THOUGHTS

Stop to think over the accomplishments in your life again.
Isn't it a great feeling to be able to look back and see how far you've come?

You Bring the Confetti, page 115

ACTIVITIES

29

30

31

RE-CAP

Faith

The Saturday Evening

POST

November 24, 1951 — 15¢

IT COST $100,000 A MINUTE—
The Story of the Great Storm of 1950

HOW CLOSE IS WAR WITH RUSSIA?
By Demaree Bess

The Lord is always with His child:
in life and death. Whether we're up or down. In our fears and worries.
Today, tomorrow. In joy or misery. For now and always.

My Favorite Verse, page 22

ACTIVITIES

1

2

3

4

5

6

7

APRIL

THOUGHTS

To accomplish anything we must have faith.
We must operate by faith from goal to goal.
We must walk by faith from day to day.
You Bring the Confetti, page 117

ACTIVITIES

8

9

10

11

12

13

14

APRIL

THOUGHTS

Faith always has an object,
and the object of our Christian faith is the Lord Jesus Christ, the Son of God,
who goes before us in every venture.
After You've Dressed for Success, page 53

ACTIVITIES

15

16

17

18

19

20

21

THOUGHTS

Be daring! Be ambitious!
You can't just wait passively hoping something great will happen to you.
You Bring the Confetti, page 115

ACTIVITIES

22

23

24

25

26

27

28

THOUGHTS

Faith is activated in direct proportion to our image of God
and our belief in His ability to make a difference in our lives.

After You've Dressed for Success, page 54

ACTIVITIES

29

30

RE-CAP

MAY

Music

All we need, to make music, is a happy heart . . .
it is the natural overflow of our spirits.

You Bring the Confetti, page 72, 73

ACTIVITIES

1

2

3

4

5

6

7

MAY

THOUGHTS

Have you ever been lifted out of depression or discouragement
by singing or hearing the great hymns of the faith?
Or called out of lethargy by listening to a magnificent symphony
by Brahms, Beethoven, or Mahler? There is power in music.

The Alchemy of the Heart, page 124

ACTIVITIES

8

9

10

11

12

13

14

THOUGHTS

Music in all its forms is a potent vehicle of human feeling and imagination.
Wide My World, Narrow My Bed, page 74

ACTIVITIES

15

16

17

18

19

20

21

MAY

T H O U G H T S

In every culture and civilization that has tread upon this earth,
the sounds of music have been at its very heart.

You Bring the Confetti, page 72

ACTIVITIES

22

23

24

25

26

27

28

MAY

THOUGHTS

You're going to solo today.
So, do it with confidence, resonance, vulnerability, and inner beauty.
People will listen with genuine pleasure. You watch their faces.

Soloing, page 20

ACTIVITIES

29

30

31

RE-CAP

JUNE

Laughter

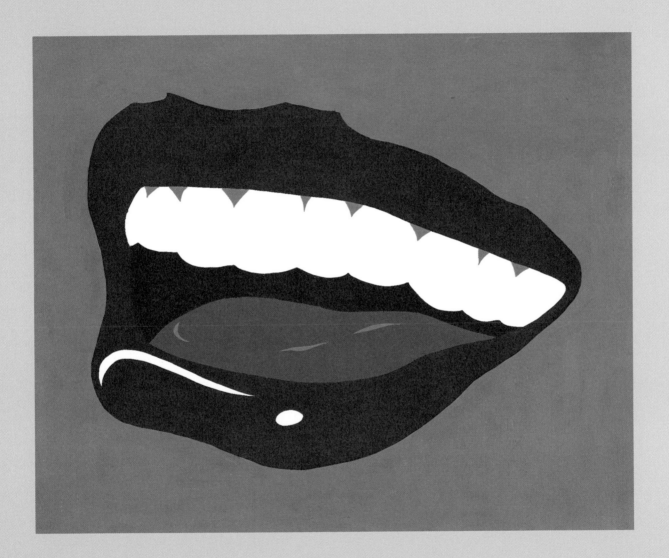

A good laugh can aid in deadening
the pain and difficulty that is frequently a part of our daily living.

Wide My World, Narrow My Bed, page 56

ACTIVITIES

1

2

3

4

5

6

7

JUNE

THOUGHTS

Let the sound of laughter ring in your ears.
Such a nice sound!

The Alchemy of the Heart, page 82

ACTIVITIES

8

9

10

11

12

13

14

THOUGHTS

In the disappointments of life, set about to create what humor you can.
It is amazing what you will come up with, and the fun you can have—all by yourself.

Wide My World, Narrow My Bed, page 58

ACTIVITIES

15

16

17

18

19

20

21

JUNE

THOUGHTS

Laugh a lot. Don't take life and your situation too seriously, or literally.
Recognize that tomorrow's another day—that bad things don't last forever.

After You've Dressed for Success, page 69

ACTIVITIES

22

23

24

25

26

27

28

THOUGHTS

Charlie Chaplin

Humor, in its many-splendored varieties, is a remarkable thing.
Henri Bergson, the French philosopher, said,
"Humor is a momentary anesthesia of the heart," and truly it is.

Wide My World, Narrow My Bed, page 56

ACTIVITIES

29

30

RE-CAP

JULY

Freedom

As we consider all that our nation has accumulated . . . in the field of
the arts, technology, medicine, philosophy, invention, and education,
there should be no end to the songs of praise we sing
for this foundation upon which we continue to build and grow.

You Bring the Confetti, page 152

ACTIVITIES

1

2

3

4

5

6

7

THOUGHTS

Becoming free is not an easy process, nor is it always an enjoyable one.
Notwithstanding those facts, there is no greater reason for living.
The process is the only thing that gives our lives substance and value.

The Alchemy of the Heart, page 182

ACTIVITIES

8

9

10

11

12

13

14

THOUGHTS

Freedom is the natural (and supernatural) by-product of God's grace.
It is the gift of God for me to be myself.

The Alchemy of the Heart, page 170

ACTIVITIES

15

16

17

18

19

20

21

JULY

THOUGHTS

Savor your independence.
You're not lonely—you're independent. There are dozens of perks to being independent.
You Bring the Confetti, page 45

ACTIVITIES

22

23

24

25

26

27

28

THOUGHTS

Freedom is an important ingredient in friendship development.
Without it, there is the very real possibility that the friendship will not endure.
Give your friend space to be free.

Wide My World, Narrow My Bed, page 128

ACTIVITIES

29

30

31

RE-CAP

AUGUST

Travel

I know of very few people who don't get excited over the prospect of a trip, even if it's only for a weekend or overnight.

The Alchemy of the Heart, page 171

ACTIVITIES

1

2

3

4

5

6

7

AUGUST

THOUGHTS

I find tremendous joy in visiting a city in which I've never been,
attempting to pick up that unique flavor which each city has.

You Bring the Confetti, page 146

ACTIVITIES

8

9

10

11

12

13

14

THOUGHTS

The wanderer is different from the person who remains at home.
He tends to be more aware of the gift of God's provision at every turn.
The wanderer is a richer person.

After You've Dressed for Success, page 31

ACTIVITIES

15

16

17

18

19

20

21

THOUGHTS

Whether we know it or not, we are all running away from something
as well as running toward something when we travel . . .
we're unconsciously seeking answers to questions we carry around with us all the time.

The Alchemy of the Heart, page 175

ACTIVITIES

22

23

24

25

26

27

28

THOUGHTS

Put twenty-five dollars aside every month for a trip.
Let it add up. Talk about your plans often.
Then when you have enough for your plane ticket—go and enjoy!

Wide My World, Narrow My Bed, page 160, 161

ACTIVITIES

29

30

31

RE-CAP

SEPTEMBER

Books

Reading brings us from darkness into light,
from ignorance to knowledge, from imprisonment to freedom.

Wide My World, Narrow My Bed, page 81

ACTIVITIES

1

2

3

4

5

6

7

SEPTEMBER

THOUGHTS

If you're going to a new job in a company . . .
read books and articles about people who have served in similar capacities.
Expect reality.

After You've Dressed for Success, page 87

ACTIVITIES

8

9

10

11

12

13

14

SEPTEMBER

THOUGHTS

Read at least one new book a month—
a classic, a new release from a favorite author, a how-to manual, a biography,
the history of a country, new scientific or theological works.

You Bring the Confetti, page 84

ACTIVITIES

15	
16	
17	
18	
19	
20	
21	

THOUGHTS

Books are like friends . . . individual, unique, and inestimable.
Wide My World, Narrow My Bed, page 81

ACTIVITIES

22

23

24

25

26

27

28

SEPTEMBER

THOUGHTS

Voices of Reason, Victory, Beauty, Faith, History, Poetry, Science . . .
reach out to instruct and encourage us from the author's pen,
and we are the better for it.

Wide My World, Narrow My Bed, page 82

ACTIVITIES

29

30

RE-CAP

OCTOBER

Solitude

Solitude is a blessing, not a curse . . .
what I glean from it now will be the food on which I am nourished
in the years to come. It will be my gift to myself for old age.

The Alchemy of the Heart, page 157, 158

ACTIVITIES

1
2
3
4
5
6
7

OCTOBER

THOUGHTS

Come apart from the routine and give your soul an unexpected perk.
You Bring the Confetti, page 42

ACTIVITIES

8

9

10

11

12

13

14

THOUGHTS

A great part of solitude was made for dreaming, gazing, drifting, floating—
anything but conscious thinking. Just be. That's enough.

The Alchemy of the Heart, page 150

ACTIVITIES

15

16

17

18

19

20

21

THOUGHTS

God is there when everybody else is off the scene . . .
nothing can ever separate us from His love.
My Favorite Verse, page 18

ACTIVITIES

22

23

24

25

26

27

28

OCTOBER

THOUGHTS

Solitude provides the space for my body to relax and regroup.
The climate for my mind to cultivate and produce.
The leisure for my spirit to discern and decide.

The Alchemy of the Heart, page 157, 158

ACTIVITIES

29

30

31

RE-CAP

NOVEMBER *Hospitality*

The size of one's home should never dictate
the outreach of one's heart.

Wide My World, Narrow My Bed, page 70

ACTIVITIES

1

2

3

4

5

6

7

NOVEMBER

THOUGHTS

Don't wait until everything is perfect before you extend hospitality.
That day will never come.
People don't come to check us out. They come to relax and have fun.

Wide My World, Narrow My Bed, page 70, 71

ACTIVITIES

8

9

10

11

12

13

14

NOVEMBER

THOUGHTS

When we reach out to others, they reach out to us.
It's a two-way street, a street practically lined with balloons and streamers
in celebration of the unique bonds of friendship.
You Bring the Confetti, page 54

ACTIVITIES

15

16

17

18

19

20

21

NOVEMBER

THOUGHTS

To entertain, we don't need to have fancy surroundings.
We don't need to own a home. We don't even need to have money.
The only thing that is required is a caring spirit.

Wide My World, Narrow My Bed, page 69

ACTIVITIES

22

23

24

25

26

27

28

NOVEMBER

THOUGHTS

Focus on the other person.
Ask questions. Exhibit genuine interest. Be informal, without a "let's get down to business" attitude.
Show that you care about other people as persons, not objects.

After You've Dressed for Success, page 94

ACTIVITIES

29

30

RE-CAP

DECEMBER

Celebrations

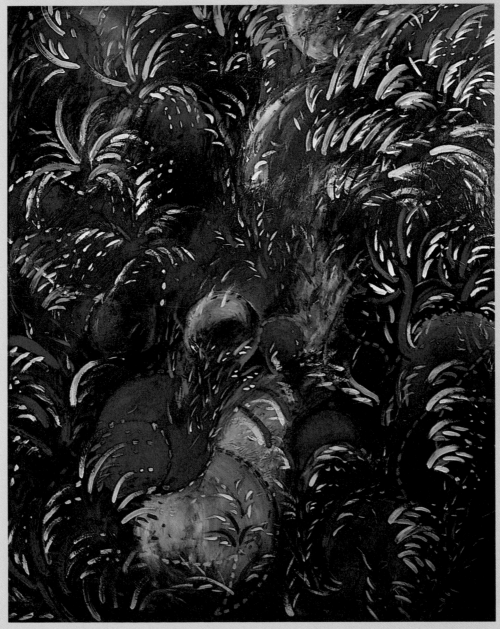

Counting our blessings gives birth to celebration.

You Bring the Confetti, page 155

ACTIVITIES

1

2

3

4

5

6

7

DECEMBER

THOUGHTS

Dream up a new reason for celebrating—
something you've not done before.
Then, develop your plans and ideas around it, invite guests, and have fun!
You Bring the Confetti, page 72

ACTIVITIES

8
9
10
11
12
13
14

T H O U G H T S

Don't always act your age.
Have fun on the job. Let some of the child in you show.
Laugh.
After You've Dressed for Success, page 51

ACTIVITIES

15

16

17

18

19

20

21

DECEMBER

THOUGHTS

Without perks our lives are easily lost in the world of money, machines, anxieties, or inertia.
Our poor, splendid souls! How they fight for food!
They have forgotten how to celebrate.

You Bring the Confetti, page 13

ACTIVITIES

22

23

24

25

26

27

28

THOUGHTS

When we are caught up in the celebration of God,
there is neither room nor time for the invasion of negative living.
You Bring the Confetti, page 154

ACTIVITIES

29	
30	
31	

RE-CAP

CREDITS

Journal Book Jacket: illustration by Janet Good.

Title page: illustration by Seymour Chwast.

January, Beauty: photo by Dennis Tannen.
photo by Dennis Tannen.
photo by Dennis Tannen.
photo by John Lawder.
illustration by Carol Fallis.

February, Friendship: photo by Steve Strickland.
photo by Dennis Tannen.
photo by John Huet.

March, Achievements: illustration by Theo Rudnak.
illustration by Terry Jenkins.
illustration by Jim Doody.
copyright by the Walt Disney Studios, reprinted with permission.

April, Faith: copyright 1951 by the Saturday Evening Post Magazine, reprinted with permission.
illustration by Janet Good.
photo by Rudi Weislein.
photo by Dennis Tannen.

May, Music: photo by Seth A. Smith, 1989
model: Josh Henry.
illustration by Steinberg.
illustration by Carol Fallis.
illustration by Penny Coltrin.
illustration by Steinberg.

June, Laughter: illustration by Terry Jenkins.
illustration by Albert M. Bender.
illustration by Terry Jenkins.

July, Freedom: sculpture / illustration by Carol Fallis.
photo by Dennis Tannen.
photo by Dennis Tannen.
illustration by Penny Coltrin.
illustration by Penny Coltrin.

August, Travel: photo by Dennis Tannen.

September, Books: illustration by Milton Glaser.

October, Solitude: photo by Dennis Tannen.
photo by Dennis Tannen.
photo by Dennis Tannen.
photo by Dennis Tannen.

November, Hospitality: sculpture / illustration by Carol Fallis.
illustration by Stevenson.

December, Celebrations: illustration by Janet Good.
illustration by Laura Cornell.
illustration by Janet Good.